True To My Heart

Spontaneous Emotions

Pramod Menon

Made with ❤ on the BookLeaf Publishing Platform

www.bookleafpub.in

www.bookleafpub.com

"To my friends, my family, and all the moments that have shaped my heart—this collection is a reflection of you. Over all these years, your love, your laughter, your challenges, and your wisdom have inspired every line. To the experiences that have carved deep within me, and to the people who made me who I am—this book is for you, True to My Heart."

Acknowledgement

The journey of creating True to My Heart has been a labor of love, and I am deeply grateful to the many people and organizations whose support and encouragement made this collection possible.

First, my sincere thanks to Bookleaf Publishing, whose professionalism, dedication, and belief in this work have been invaluable. Their commitment to bringing this book to life with such care and attention to detail has been truly humbling, and I am honored to have partnered with them in this endeavor.

A special note of appreciation goes to Anup Kumar K, my colleague, and dear friend. Anup's creativity and artistic vision have brought this book's cover to life in a way I could never have imagined. His contribution to this book, both in his artistry and his friendship, has been a gift beyond measure.

To my family and friends, thank you for your love, patience, and understanding as I poured my heart into these poems. Your encouragement and unwavering support have kept me grounded through every high and low. Your belief in me is what has made this collection possible.

Finally, to everyone who has read, shared, or connected with my poetry over the years—your voices and stories have been woven into the fabric of these pages. I write not just for myself, but for all of us who seek meaning, who search for truth, and who find beauty in life's complexities.

Thank you all for being part of this journey.

Pramod Menon

Preface

True to My Heart is a collection of poems that spans over three decades of personal growth, love, loss, and discovery. Writing has always been my way of making sense of the world; an intimate act of unraveling thoughts and emotions, of turning fleeting moments into something permanent. These poems are fragments of my heart and figments of my imagination, each one a snapshot of the experiences that have shaped me, the people who have touched my life, and the quiet epiphanies that have emerged in the stillness of my thoughts.

When I look back over these years, I can see the Metamorphosis and the Catalysts of Change. There are moments of joy so intense they seem to shine with a light of their own, and there are shadows of sorrow that remind me how fragile and precious life truly is. In these poems, you'll find reflections of both—the highs and the lows, the love I've given and received, and the spaces in between where I've learned to find myself.

The title "True to My Heart" captures the essence of this journey. These poems are not simply a record of events; they are an exploration of the heart's depth, the ways it bends and breaks, heals and soars. They are true to my heart not just in the sense that they reflect my own experiences, but in the way they strive to speak to something universal—the way we all search for meaning, connection, and authenticity in our lives.

Over the past thirty years, I have written through seasons of change—through the bloom of new beginnings and the pangs of painful endings. These poems are my attempt to honor those experiences, to give voice to the emotions that often go unspoken, and to share the quiet wisdom I've gathered along the way. They are for anyone who has ever felt the pull of their own heart, who has navigated the shifting tides of life, or who has ever wondered where the next step might lead.

Each poem here is a piece of me, yet I hope they resonate with something larger than myself. I offer them as an invitation to reflect, to feel, and to remember that even in the most uncertain moments, we are always true to our hearts.

Thank you for reading. May these words speak to you in ways both unexpected and familiar, just as they have spoken to me through the years.

Pramod Menon

Last respects and ever lasting respect!

Adieu to the great Teacher, who enlightened
many a mind,
Through simple living and high thinking,
A Great Guru, Guide and a Philosopher,
A Tall man, Taller Thoughts and a True
Karma Yogi,
A Teacher who trusted my inane talent,
Honed my skills through constant guidance,
Instilled the courage to pursue my dreams,
Relentlessly with grit and gumption.
A Teacher who truly blessed me "A Bright
and Prosperous Life",
Inspired me to "fearlessly pursue new
Heights"
Has bid adieu to mere mortals and mortality,
And embraced enlightened immortality.

A tribute to Panicker Sir, the greatest
Teacher!

The Pied Pipers

The Pied Piper and his magical music,
The enchanting and enticing story,
Of the mice and the wice that feasted on,
The divide and deceit in the middle age!

The current world and its currency,
The decay over the decades,
The disbelief and the dismay of many,
The worst nightmares and the stark realities!

The realistic realms of reality,
Manipulation of minds and mandates,
The "fake" facts and the facade,
The brutal betrayal of conscience.

The eternal greed and the divide,
Broken Promises and the silent screams,
The lingering restlessness,
The lull before the looming storms.

Shades and Shadows

The green shades,
The lingering shadows,
The moonlit night,
And the ruminating mind!

The exotic nightfall,
The serene setting,
The tranquil mind,
And the spontaneous emotions ...

Messi, the Messiah!

A man with the golden left foot,
In an in-equal, "right" world"!
He has "left" the biggest stage,
Leaving immortal memories.

Mere mortals run after a ball,
The Messiah made the world -
Revolve around the same ball.
What more can be a revolution!

Maradona inspired a generation,
"Left" an indelible Impression,
Igniting Messi, the Messiah,
That's the true "Hand of God".

Winning against all odds,
And the righteous "Naysayers",
Leaving an eternal Hope,
And Dreams that don't Die!

Maradona: Player from Another Planet!

Of course, he made mistakes,
And he paid for them.
But the ball didn't gather dirt,
It is still pristine and pure!

His success was due to hard work,
And luck had nothing to do with it!
He was "Black" or "White" and never "Grey",
He had "Guts" and "Character" to take a
stand and say so!

Messi said even if I played for a million years,
I'd never come close to Maradona!
Not that I'd want to anyway,
As he's the greatest there's ever been!

Platini said What Zidane could do with a ball,
Maradona could do with an Orange!
Zico said, he saw Maradona do things

That God himself would doubt were
possible!!

Maradona said Poverty is bad, it's difficult,
and he knew it well,
You want a lots of things and all you can do is
to dream,
Would be nice if there were more justice, if
those who have a lot,
Had a little less and those who have a little,
had a little more!

Adieu to the one and only Maradona..........

Dawn and Dusk

The dwindling twilight,
And the nocturnal charm!
The lingering shadows,
And the sultry evenings!

Tall trees, taller shadows,
Small men and shallow minds,
Games, gambles and goof ups,
Hide 'n' seek of Dawn 'n' Dusk!

A free ride

Injecting Hope,
Like a Dope,
You get High,
And do feel Good!

Reality is Different,
Not many Realize,
Scoff at Rationale,
And wait for the last laugh!

Admire the Flight,
Of hot air Balloons,
Enjoy the free Ride,
Till the Beginning of the End!

Ramble in the Rubble

The lush green fields,
The golden growth!
Unseen sweat and toil,
Of the faceless folks!!

The universal suffering,
Of hunger and privation!
Not an issue of charity,
But an issue of justice!!

For the passerby,
Just a sight to behold!
For the hands that feed,
A way of life and not just livelihood!!

COVID'19 - A great realization!

A pandemic that put things in perspective,
Showed how mortal, we truly are!
Pricked a lot of hot air balloons,
Mocked all boundaries and borders!!

The less, that is said, the better,
Of the walls, that we built all around!
To hide, block, ban and boast,
Till the avalanche had the last laugh!!

A catastrophe sans discrimination,
A tranquilliser that bust all markets!
That opened the eyes of humanity,
To understand and appreciate Life!!

Normalcy, though a distant dream,
Will dawn with new normals, facts and fiction!
Soon, we will resort to and restore,
The old ways, as old habits die hard!!

Black and White!

Experiments with Truth,
Experience of the Truth,
Shades of grey and true lies,
Circus full of colourful characters.

Facts, stranger than fiction,
Fusion, a poisonous concoction,
Emotions, sinister manipulations,
People, the sacrificial pawns!

History, the ever repeated story,
Lessons, that are never learnt,
Wounds, that are never healed,
Hounds, the architects of the holocaust!

Comrades and Camaraderie

It's been twenty years in the Garden City,
What a ride it's been so far,
Humble beginnings and a billion dreams,
True comrades and strong bonds.

The cherished friendship and camaraderie,
Augustus beginning in August'98!
Transience of all things material, reminds us,
That the Journey itself has been the reward!

Making of a Man

The Mortality of Revolutionary Life,
The Immortality of the Cause,
The Reward for doing the Right,
The Clean and Clear Conscience.

The Courage and the Consequences,
The Character and the Uncompromising
Integrity,
The Greater Cause and the Evergreen Values,
The real Raw Life Experiences and the
Unknown, that maketh a MAN.............

Satirical Riddles

Change sans Progress,
Revolution sans Evolution,
Commitment sans Conscience,
Solitude sans Tranquility.

Bond sans Bonding,
Message sans Meaning,
Journey sans Destination,
Interesting and Enigmatic Ironies ...

A Tribute to Teachers & Mentors

To be an eternal inquisitive student,
In the amazing University of Life!
To have great minds as Mentors,
In a complex and cluttered world.
In a world full of superficiality,
Where people master the art of artificiality,
Inspiring people to be true to oneself,
And to be genuine, fearless and humane.
To instill the courage to confront,
Uncertainty, Ignorance and Fear of Failure,
To inspire to follow one's heart,
To Change the World, ain't it a Tall Charter?!

Sincere thanks to my Teachers and
Mentors........

Dreams, Desire and Ignited Minds...

Adieu to the man who ignited many a mind,
Through simple living and high thinking,
A Great Guide and a Genuine Guru,
An Eternal Dreamer and a True KarmaYogi,
A grounded, mild mannered man,
With a humane and humble background,
Became the "Rocket Man" of India,
Through inspiring innovations,
Ignited many a mind to dream and dream
more!
The man with the Wings of Fire,
Has now embarked on a new Journey,
Sans the company of mere mortals...

A tribute to Dr. APJ Kalam....

Soulful Solitude

The Chemistry of Friendship,
The Commonness of Minds,
The Colourful Camaraderie,
And the True celebration of Life.

The Absence of Expectations,
Caveats and Compromise,
The Confidence to Confide,
And the True reflection of Life.

The Pain, Pangs and Promise,
The Learnings and Leanings,
The True Trust sans Tests,
The Eloquent Silence and the Soulful
Solitude!

Freedom - A Warning & A Deadline!

To quote Rousseau "Man is born free; And everywhere he is in chains"!
Irony of Bonds and Bondage,
The Past, Present and the Future,
Enigma of Freedom to be Free,
And the journey from the Womb to the Tomb!!

Pramod Menon
Inspired by the movie "Munnariyippu" - "A Warning" and "A Deadline"!

Eternal Gratitude

The lighthouse of hope,
The unwavering faith,
The right direction,
The light of reason......

The focus and passion,
The art as well as science,
The call of duty,
The clear conscience......

The guide and the God,
The good and the bad,
The right and the wrong,
The friend and the philosopher ......

The founder and the foundation,
The values, victories and wins,
The epitome of eternal optimism,
Teacher, the master of all ....

Courage to Fail

Power of dreams,
And the restlessness,
The fuel to travel,
To the Promised Land!
Thirst for knowledge,
And the relentless pursuit,
To study for dignity,
And not just for degree!
Take a stand for what's just,
And listen to the inner voice,
Dreams remain as dreams,
Lest you have courage to fail!

To be or not to be

The rights and the wrongs,
Idealism and opportunism,
Speak up or to swallow,
Confront or to conform!
The values and the price,
Beliefs and the bias,
Stand up or to salute,
Dignity or decadence!

The conscience and the commerce,
Meaningful life or menial life,
Family and friends or fear of foes,
Self-confidence or slavery!
The road taken or the road not taken,
Candid and confident or compromise,
Create history or just be a story,
I chose to be myself and to Play to Win.

Dreams Never Die

Yesterday was a dream,
Today, a burning reality,
Tomorrow, a mystic mirage,
Life goes on, in the flickering hope,
And the flashing nostalgia.
Look back and recollect,
Recapture the golden moments,
The bliss of childhood,
The blooming blunders,
And the follies of the youth!
Those days are over forever.
Life was a poem sans words....
In this world full of baffling contrasts,
And the violent uncertainties,
In this age of opiates and oracles,
Sedatives and sputniks, drugs and dreams,
Pulls of poverty and the pressures of
prosperity,
Life goes on due to dreams that never die!

Being Samson,
Sanju Samson

The power brokers and deal makers,
Loitering at the corridors of cricket,
Deemed and decided to block, blame and
banish,
A one of its kind of talent who puts team first
always,
Not for one or two years but for at least a
decade!

Despite many illustrious cricket experts,
mostly foreign,
Vouching for his exceptional and explosive
talent,
But call up to the national team was elusive
for many years,
Then the tactics was to include in the
selection,

But exclude from the Playing Eleven,
Or select, include in the playing eleven for
one or two games,
Then drop irrespective of his performance,
Strategy was too good to create a narrative,
Have given 20 - 30 games but he lacks
consistency,
The stories and narratives were always one
sided,
Thirty games in how many years?

A decade and yardsticks were always different
for him,
Call it bias, bigotry or blindness,
Justice was not just delayed but denied!

Things took a different turn, though late,
When the coach and captain backed him and
provided clarity,
He rose from his own ashes like a phoenix,
To stand up, deliver and outstanding
centuries,
Three in Seven games and made the deaf hear
and the blind see!

When talent is denied their opportunities,
The loss is not just personal, it is a loss for the
entire world,
Such gross injustice and neglect,
Hope it's not meted out again and again,
Not just Samson, the one and only Sanju
Samson,
But no talent deserves such a raw treatment!
This ain't cricket, the gentleman's game!!

Adieu to Raman Lamba

That tragic hit : From coma to full stop,
It was only a matter of time.
But that direct hit of fate,
Was premature and cruel.

Though he died so young,
With many unfulfilled dreams....
He will always be remembered,
For his swashbuckling style.

Of all fields that his death,
Happened to be on a cricket field,
Makes it more sad and tragic -
For it just ain't cricket!